Country Kitchen Charm
Charm COLORING BOOK

TERESA GOODRIDGE

DOVER PUBLICATIONS
GARDEN CITY, NEW YORK

Full of irresistible charm, this unique book celebrates the "heart of the home" with a delightful variety of 31 ready-to-color illustrations. The beautifully detailed images include kitchen designs ranging from rustic farmhouse to chic modern, all accented with lovely furnishings, pretty table settings, quaint collectibles, herb gardens, baked goods, and more! Enjoy coloring with markers, colored pencils, or any medium of your choice. Plus, the pages are perforated and printed on one side only for easy removal and display.

Copyright

Copyright © 2022 by Dover Publications
All rights reserved.

Bibliographical Note

Country Kitchen Charm Coloring Book is a new work,
first published by Dover Publications in 2022.

International Standard Book Number

ISBN-13: 978-0-486-84892-1
ISBN-10: 0-486-84892-2

Manufactured in the United States of America
84892202   2022
www.doverpublications.com

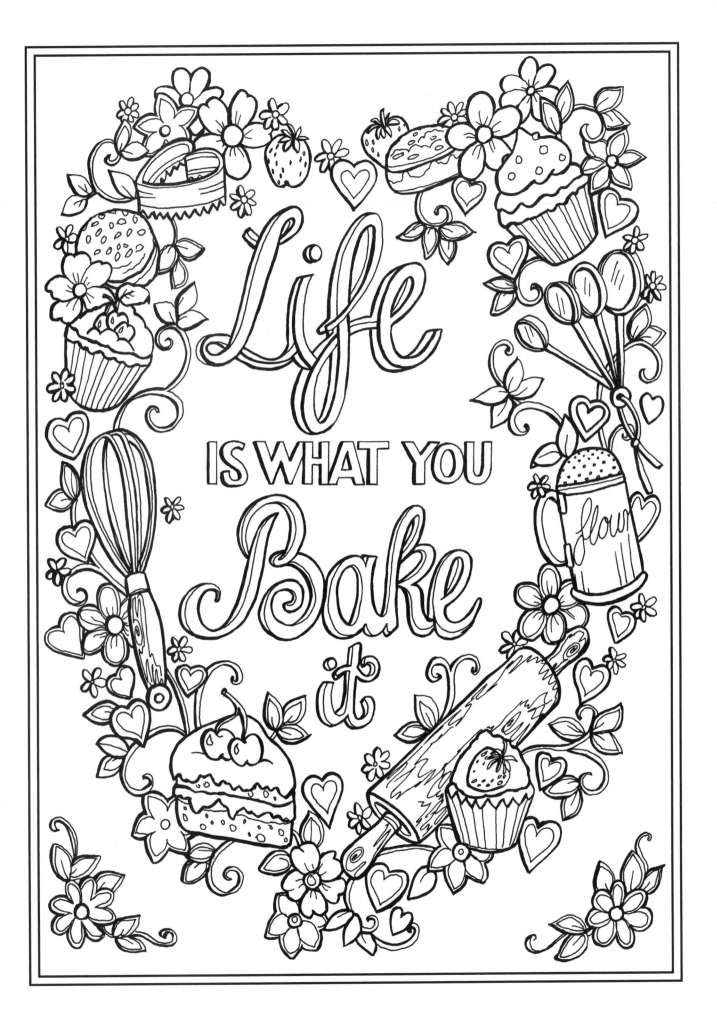

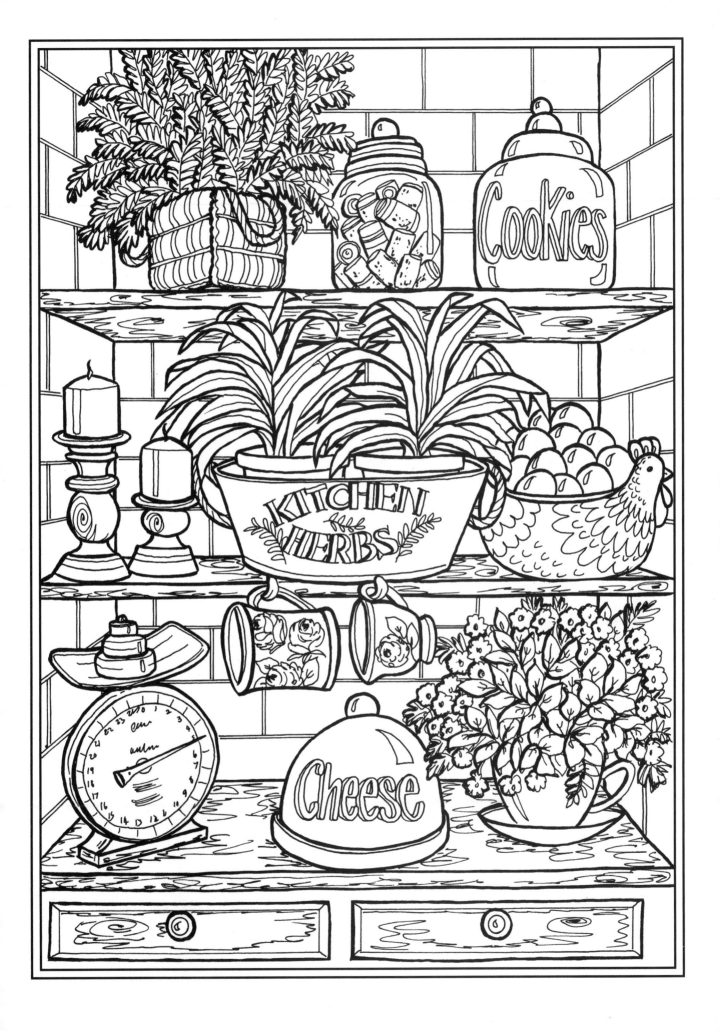

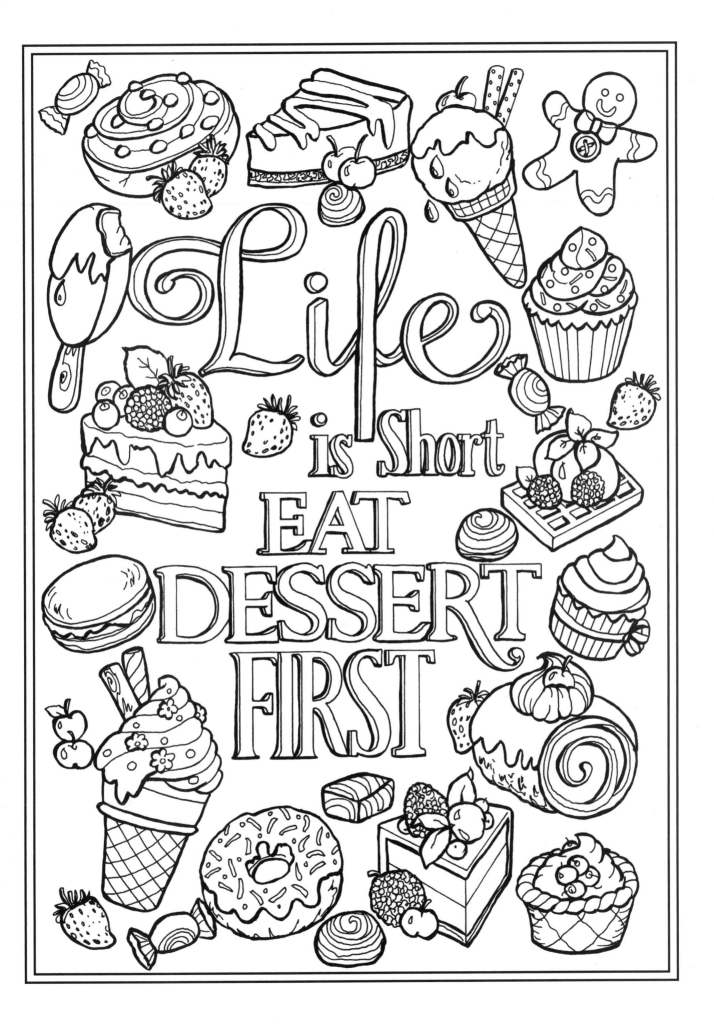